To:

Libby

From:

Sherrie

Date:

Dec. 2011

Waves of God's Healing

Artwork by
D. Morgan ®

Carol Hamblet Adams

H ®

HARVEST HOUSE PUBLISHERS

EUGENE, OREGON

Waves of God's Healing

Text Copyright © 2011 by Carol Hamblet Adams
Artwork Copyright © 2011 by D. Morgan

Published by Harvest House Publishers
Eugene, Oregon 97402
www.harvesthousepublishers.com

ISBN: 978-0-7369-2438-2

Design and production by Garborg Design Works, Savage, Minnesota

Printed in Malaysia

11 12 13 14 15 16 17 / IM / 10 9 8 7 6 5 4 3 2 1

Dedication

To my treasured family, Kristin and
Mike, Amanda and Kevin, Maura
and Todd...and to my relatives and
friends, whose faith, love, support, and prayers
have been constant waves of healing in my life.

Acknowledgments

To Etta Wilson and Jean Christen for
believing in me...and to Harvest House,
for helping to bring God's healing light and
love to the world through the written word.

A Word from Carol

I have had a lifelong love of the ocean. Going to God's shore has always brought me peace, no matter how turbulent the waves of my life have been.

For years, as I sat in my trusted old blue canvas beach chair, with my toes wiggled down in the sand, I would notice one thing—the constant ebb and flow of the ocean. Whether my life was stormy or calm, I could always depend on the persistent, unceasing rhythm of the waves. Like a steadfast friend, the waves were always there, reaching out to embrace the shoreline… and me.

One day I realized that the never-ending pulse of the waves is no different from the never-ending beat of God's love. No matter what I am experiencing in my life, no matter how whole or broken I am, no matter whether I feel close to God or far away, God is always present…waiting to come into my life…to heal me with His love…His peace…His strength…His comfort. The Waves of God's Love will never cease. All I have to do is be still…listen to them…and receive them.

It is my hope and my prayer that you will experience the Waves of God's Love and Healing through this little book. May you feel yourself at the ocean…being refreshed and renewed by God's healing waters.

Wave of Healing

Morning has broken on the beach. I come here today…to this sacred place, needing healing in my life. I am frightened about tomorrow and consumed with worry. I feel broken in mind and in spirit. I am having a hard time concentrating on anything because my future seems so uncertain. As a brilliant yellow sun bursts over the horizon, I notice an old beach chair lying in the sand. It calls me to rest.

Lord, You know the tears I have shed…the cries for help I have uttered…the need I have to be healed. Help me remember that You are our ultimate Healer…our great Physician. Help me place my trust in You. Please send Your Wave of Healing and restore my mind, body, and spirit to wholeness again. Thank You for the gift of this beach chair. May I rest in it as I rest in Your love, knowing that You are my heavenly Father and want only what is best for me and those in my life. Thank You for the morning's beautiful sunrise. Help me always feel the warmth of Your healing love.

"Thus says the LORD… I have heard your prayer and seen your tears. I will heal you."

—2 KINGS 20:5

Wave of Forgiveness

*I*t is a beautiful day on the shore this morning. The wind is blowing through the beach grasses and stirring up the blue-green waters. As far as I can see, there are rows and rows of white-capped waves rolling in toward the shore. Yet I am here today with my spirit crushed by the hurtful words and actions of others. I feel anger in my heart toward those who have wronged me. Resentment seems to consume me. As I watch the waves come in, one after another, I see a beautiful shell tossed onto the shore. I pick up the little shell and hold it tightly in my hand.

Lord, I come to You on the shore once again because I am hurting and don't want to live with anger in my heart anymore. Please send Your Wave of Forgiveness to wash over me and mend my wounded pride. Teach me to let go of any resentment I feel and replace bitterness with love. As I watch the waves constantly reach out to hug the shore, I ask You to help me reach out and embrace those who have wronged me. Just as the ocean brings me beautiful shells, I ask You to bring me the solace of forgiveness in my heart.

"Forgive whatever grievances you have against one another. Forgive as the Lord has forgiven you."

—COLOSSIANS 3:13

9

Wave of Courage

As I come to the ocean on this warm summer day, doubt and uncertainty seem to overwhelm me. A difficult situation is facing me now, and I wonder how I can be brave enough for myself and for those who need me. I wonder if I will ever be able to find the courage to persevere amidst my pain. I notice a brightly colored beach umbrella nearby, sheltering someone from the hot sun. Looking at it, I feel the overwhelming protective power of God.

Lord, I am feeling timid and afraid today. Please send Your Wave of Courage to calm my fears. Thank You for the gift of this beautiful umbrella. It reminds me that You are always over me…to protect me…and to shelter me from harm. Thank You for always assuring me that if I rely on You, I can and will be brave enough to face my difficult situation…and courageous enough to stand tall…and make it through.

"Even though I walk in the dark valley I fear no evil; for you are at my side with your rod and staff that give me courage."

—Psalm 23:4

Wave of Trust

It is a crystal-clear day here at the beach this morning. The wind is blowing gently. I come reflecting on the uncertainty that has filled my life lately. I have many serious concerns about myself and my loved ones. I want us all to be safe and well. I want to be assured that everything will work out fine. But many situations have me very worried. And as hard as I may try to control things, I realize I can't. Out on the horizon, a beautiful boat is moving slowly in the distance, its sails billowing in the wind.

Lord, as I stand here on Your sandy shore, I am feeling very anxious and concerned. Please send Your Wave of Trust today, to wash over me and take away my doubt. Thank You for the gift of this beautiful sailboat. Help me be like this vessel and allow You to take over the steering wheel of my life. Help me trust, not in myself, but in You for direction. Give me the confidence to let go and allow You to lead the way. Help me know that if I trust in You and allow You to be in charge, I will always be safe and will always find my way home.

"Trust in the LORD with all your heart, and lean not on your own understanding."

—PROVERBS 3:5

12

Wave of Strength

It is late afternoon on this overcast day as I come to the shore. The sea is dark, just as my life has seemed lately. Much is being asked of me, and I wonder if I have the strength to survive. I am uncertain about decisions I have to make…and I am tired from the stress of my concerns. As I stand here at the ocean's edge, the water reaches out and wraps its white foam around my ankles. Then it recedes. Glancing down on the sand, I notice a beautiful beach stone, tossed ashore by the waves. I reach down and pick it up.

Lord, You know the doubt and uncertainty I have been feeling, wondering if I can do what is being asked of me. I know I am too weak to do everything alone. Please send Your Wave of Strength to wash over me...to fill me and renew me. Help assure me that with You "all things are possible" (Matthew 19:26). Thank You for the gift of this little beach stone...for reminding me that You are my rock...always there for me to lean on...and to supply the strength for my journey. I, too, have been tossed...but through the storms, You always wash me...polish me...and bring me to the shore again.

"In him who is the source of my strength I have strength for everything."

—PHILIPPIANS 4:13

15

Wave of Hope

*I*t is a cloudy afternoon as I come to the shore again. Just as clouds fill the sky, clouds seem to fill my life…clouds of uncertainty and doubt. Lately my life has been difficult. I have felt so weary and discouraged. So often my prayers seem to go unanswered. Many times I feel like giving up. I glance out at the ocean and see a tall lighthouse in the distance… shining its bright glow across the water.

Lord, I come seeking Your help once again. You promise me hope in the midst of my trials, yet I experience despair. Please send Your Wave of Hope to wash over my tired, weary body. Thank You for the gift of this lighthouse. Just as ships look to its bright signal to protect them and keep them out of harm's way, may I keep my eyes on Your light, knowing that You are always there to protect me and keep me safe from the storm. Your light will always be my beacon in the darkness…shining brightly to take away my despair and to offer me hope for a promising tomorrow.

"They that hope in the LORD will renew their strength, they will soar as with eagle's wings; they will run and not grow weary, walk and not grow faint."

—ISAIAH 40:31

Wave of Patience

$\mathcal{I}$t is dusk on this beautiful evening. As I walk to the water, I see the sun going down slowly over the horizon, painting a magnificent seascape of vivid reds and yellows. So much has been happening in my life lately that I am feeling uneasy and impatient. I have become very restless waiting for answers to so many questions. It feels good to come to the shore and just take a little time out. I notice a fisherman standing on the shore in front of me and watch as he brings his pole back and gracefully casts his line out into the ocean time and time again.

Lord, as I stand on Your shore tonight, You know how anxious I have been lately, wanting immediate answers to so many questions. It has been very hard for me to wait. I ask You to please send Your Wave of Patience to heal my restless mind. Help me be like this fisherman…who waits patiently to feel the tug on his line. Help me lean on You as I wait for answers…knowing that in Your time, You will bring resolution to my questions and provide all that I need.

"Be patient under trial. Persevere in prayer."

—Romans 12:12

Wave of Peace

I come to the ocean today in the early morning. Roaring waves spill onto the shore as a lazy sun begins to appear in the sky. I sit on the cool sand and stretch my legs out. There is such peace here at the shore...something I want so much in my life. Yet sleep escapes me, and troubles seem to preoccupy my thoughts. I have been worried lately and no longer have peace in my heart. In the hush of the early morning, I see a lone seagull flying gracefully in the sky. I watch as it soars and dips above the churning waters...seemingly without a care in the world.

Lord, as I sit here on Your shore this morning, You know the anxiety in my heart. Please send Your Wave of Peace to wash away my doubts and worries. Thank You for sending this beautiful seagull to me today. Help me give You all of my cares and concerns so that I may be set free like this bird. Help me realize true peace can only come from You. Thank You for reassuring me that I am in Your hands...and that if I rely on You, I will come through the storms of my life and find true peace in You.

"Dismiss all anxiety from your minds. Present your needs to God in every form of prayer and in petitions full of gratitude. Then God's own peace, which is beyond all understanding, will stand guard over your hearts and minds in Christ Jesus."

—PHILIPPIANS 4:6

Wave of Comfort

A gentle rain is falling as I come to the beach today in my yellow slicker. Rain has come into my life too…sorrow has been heavy on my heart. I come to the ocean again…seeking comfort for my pain…consolation for my loss…and solace for my grief. As I feel the wet drops on my face, I am reminded that it takes rain to make a rainbow…that tears mean we have been blessed to love…and that God can and does brighten all of our hearts when we turn to Him. I look down and watch as three little sandpipers scurry along the sand, searching for food and dodging the waves that dance at the shoreline.

Lord, *You know the grief that has been weighing heavily on my heart. Please send Your Wave of Comfort to wash over me and lift me in my time of sorrow. Thank You for walking with me through my pain…for sending this gentle rain…that reminds me that Your tears are falling along with mine. Thank You, too, for these little sandpipers that comfort my heart and remind me that I am never alone. Thank You for these brief joy-filled moments that ease my pain…and reassure me that You will lift the rain and bring the sun to my life again.*

"Come to me, all you who are weary and find life burdensome and I will refresh you. Take my yoke upon your shoulders and learn from me, for I am gentle and humble of heart. Your souls will find rest, for my yoke is easy and my burden light."

—MATTHEW 11:28

23

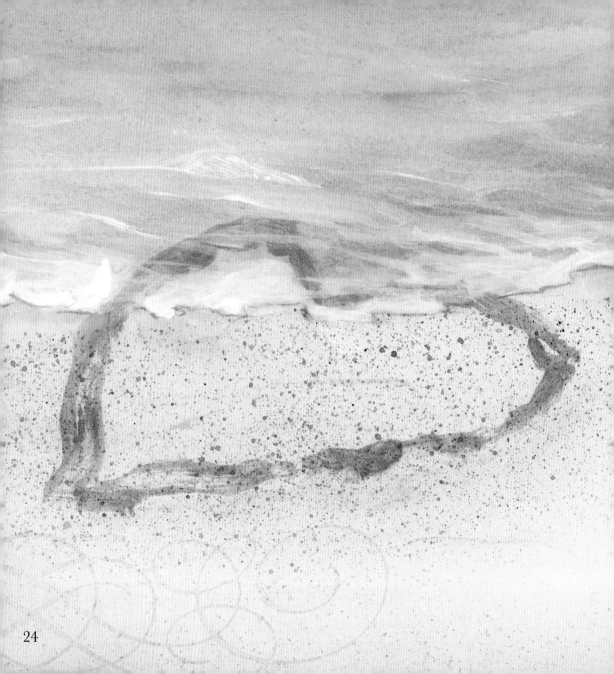

Wave of Love

It is slightly overcast today as I walk along the shore. My heart has been sad lately…and I have been feeling very alone. Relationships have been difficult…love has seemed very distant in my life. I know how important it is to both give and receive love, but recently I have been feeling empty and drained of emotion. As I walk the beach, I come to a big heart that someone has drawn in the sand with a stick. Soon the tide will stretch out its arms and erase this beautiful heart…but it touches me and reminds me of God's never-ending love.

Lord, what a blessing to be on Your shore again today. Thank You for this unexpected gift of a heart in the sand…which reminds me of Your all-embracing love. Please send Your Wave of Love to wash over me and cleanse me of any feelings of unworthiness…so I may once again be able to give and receive affection. Help me always know how precious I am in Your sight, for I was made in Your image and likeness. Thank You for touching my life with so many people who care…and for opening me to love myself and others again.

"I trust in the steadfast love of God forever and ever."

—Psalm 52:8

Wave of Gratitude

It is evening as I walk to the shore. The ocean is incredibly calm…there is hardly a ripple in sight. The water seems so quiet and tranquil…so still…so undisturbed. I stop to sit on the sand and reflect on my life, with its many ups and downs. Yet, through it all, I know the Lord has walked with me every step of the way. I look nearby and see a beautiful sandcastle…and I am reminded again of the many gifts You give me every single day.

Lord, as I come to the shore tonight, I ask that You always help me come to You…not only in times of trouble, but even when my world is calm, like the ocean tonight. Please send Your Wave of Gratitude so I may always see the many blessings You give me. Heal any ungratefulness I may have, so I may always live a life full of thankfulness. Help me look at this playful sandcastle and remember to cherish my blessings every single moment, before they are washed away. Remind me that even in the midst of trials, I can still be ever thankful for the many blessings You continue to shower upon me.

"O Lord, my God, forever will I give You thanks."

—Psalm 30:13

Wave of Faith

It is stormy out today. The white-capped waves seem to be raging all around me. I feel as if I have been in rough waters too, drowning in a sea of despair. I have even begun to wonder where God is in the midst of my pain. Sometimes it is hard to continue having faith when everything in my life seems so hard. As I watch the crashing waves, I notice a little red buoy…bobbing up and down over the whitecaps. I gaze at it…mesmerized by its ability to ride out the turbulence.

Lord, You know so well the rough time I am going through now. Please send Your Wave of Faith today to heal my doubt. Help lift me up so that I may believe in You again. Help me be like this little red buoy. Anchor me in faith so deeply and so strongly that I, too, may keep my head above life's rough waters. Help me remain steadfast in my faith. And even when I have trouble believing, help me know that You are in the middle of every storm…to calm the seas…to wipe my tears…and to keep me safe from the raging waters.

"Do not let your hearts be troubled. Have faith in God and faith in me."

—John 14:1

Wave of Joy

I come to the ocean today in late afternoon. The beach is empty, but signs of the day are scattered everywhere. I walk by a child's pail and shovel that probably were used to build sandcastles earlier in the day…or perhaps carried treasures found on the shore. I listen to the pounding surf and feel a pounding in my heart. Sadness has been part of my life for so long that I have forgotten what it is like to be a child again…to smile…to laugh…to feel even a glimmer of joy.

Lord, *I want so much to find joy in the little gifts You sprinkle throughout my days. But You know I have let burdens overtake my life. Please send Your Wave of Joy to wash over me. Refresh and renew my spirit so that I have eyes again to see the joy all around me. Thank You for sending this little pail and shovel today…for teaching me that happiness and delight come in small pleasures. Thank You for being faithful to me…for brightening my spirit…for restoring joy to my heart. Thank You for teaching me to dance…to smile…and to sing again.*

"He will fill your mouth with laughter, and your lips with rejoicing."

—JOB 8:21

A sliver of the
moon hangs in the early morning sky
as the sun wakes up to a sleeping world and peeks over the horizon.

My footsteps are the first on the beach today…

A new beginning…

A new day to feel more Waves of God's Healing.

About the Author

Carol Hamblet Adams is a writer, a motivational speaker, and the author of *My Beautiful Broken Shell: Words of Hope to Refresh the Soul*. She gives keynotes, workshops, retreats, and bereavement seminars. Carol's life centers around her faith, her family, her friends, and God's magnificent shore. She lives on beautiful Cape Cod and can be found beachcombing on its sandy beaches or swimming in its blue-green waters. She can be reached at carolhambletadams@comcast.net or at www.carolhambletadams.com.